relationships
workbook

Resources by Les and Leslie Parrott

Books

Becoming Soul Mates
Getting Ready for the Wedding
Like a Kiss on the Lips
The Marriage Mentor Manual
Questions Couples Ask
Relationships
Relationships Workbook
Saving Your Marriage Before It Starts
Saving Your Marriage Before It Starts Workbook for Men
Saving Your Marriage Before It Starts Workbook for Women

Video Curriculum

Saving Your Marriage Before It Starts
Mentoring Engaged and Newlywed Couples

Audio Pages

Relationships
Saving Your Marriage Before It Starts

Books by Les Parrott III

High Maintenance Relationships
Love's Unseen Enemy
Seven Secrets of a Healthy Dating Relationship

relationships
workbook

An Open and Honest Guide to
Making Bad Relationships Better
and Good Relationships Great

Drs. Les & Leslie Parrott

ZondervanPublishingHouse

Grand Rapids, Michigan

A Division of HarperCollins*Publishers*

Relationships Workbook
Copyright © 1998 by Les and Leslie Parrott

Requests for information should be addressed to:

🏭 ZondervanPublishingHouse
Grand Rapids, Michigan 49530

ISBN: 0-310-22438-1

Printed in the United States of America

98 99 00 01 02 03 04 /❖ DC/ 10 9 8 7 6 5 4 3

Contents

How to Use This Workbook

Too often, reading a book can lead to great ideas, but little action. This workbook is meant to change all that. Its self-tests and exercises will help you put feet on the ideas you have while reading *Relationships*. And we believe you'll enjoy it. As Shakespeare said, "Joy's soul lies in the doing."

While this workbook will become a rather personal record of your own exploration—and while it is designed to be used on your own—we have also written it to be used in group settings. In other words, you may want to do the self-tests and exercises while reading each chapter on your own, and then take time to discuss the questions with others after completing the chapter (this makes for a convenient nine- or ten-week classroom or small-group series). Interacting with others on this material will not only help you compare and contrast your varying viewpoints, it will help you better define and articulate your own perspective.

Each chapter contains four specific self-tests or exercises to tap into a particular idea you are reading about. We suggest pausing as you make your way through each chapter and doing the recommended exercises at that particular time. Following the four chapter exercises are a half-dozen discussion questions for small groups. Each section concludes with suggestions for further study of the chapter's topic by recommending other relationship resources.

As you work through the pages of this book, make it your own. Don't get too hung up on following the rules. If a particular exercise leads your down a more intriguing path, take it. Some of these exercises may simply serve as springboards to discussions that more appropriately fit your style. However, if an exercise seems a bit challenging, don't give up on it. As the saying goes, anything worth having is worth working for. In any case, we pray you will enjoy your journey toward making bad relationships better and good relationships great.

Les and Leslie Parrott
Center for Relationship Development
Seattle Pacific University

exercises

for

chapter one

The Compulsion
for Completion

Your Relational Readiness

The following self-test will take about five minutes and will help you assess your relational "readiness." Answer each item by using the following scale to indicate the degree to which it is true for you:

> 4 — Often
> 3 — Sometimes
> 2 — Rarely
> 1 — Never

_____ I feel a sense of relief when I don't have to be alone.

_____ Any relationship is better than nothing.

_____ If I'm not in a dating relationship, I feel less desirable.

_____ I experience a little bit of panic when I think of not having someone to be close to.

_____ The very idea of solitude strikes fear in my heart.

_____ I'm tempted to settle for most any relationship because I don't know if I can find anyone better.

_____ My romantic relationships are more of an issue of being selected rather than doing the selecting.

_____ When I am dating someone else I feel better about myself.

_____ I don't like to be alone.

_____ I don't have a very clear idea of the personal qualities I look for in a person to date or even to be friends with.

_____ Total Score

Scoring: Add the numbers you have placed beside each item. There is a possible total of forty points. To interpret your score, use the following scale:

40–30 A score in this range is a strong indicator of your need to establish a healthier sense of your identity and personal wholeness. You will want to pay special attention to the four steps toward wholeness discussed in this chapter.

29–20 A score in this range indicates that you have done some significant work in establishing a healthy identity and a good sense of self-worth.

You still have more work to do, however, in constructing an integrated and whole sense of self that will help to ensure healthier relationships.

19–1   A score in this range indicates an established sense of security in who you are and a confident perspective on your sense of personal wholeness. This should serve you well in your relationships.

Healing Your Primal Pain

This exercise can take as little as fifteen minutes to much longer and will require a place for quite contemplation and self-exploration. You may want to use additional paper for this exercise.

- Reflect on your personal history and make note of any memories you have of feeling abandoned or neglected (even if they seem fairly insignificant).

_____

_____

_____

_____

- Are there people from your past or present that you blame for not being there for you? Who are they and what do you blame them for?

_____

_____

_____

_____

- As you review these painful moments from your past, do you see ways in which they may still be impacting your present? In what ways are they determining choices you are making when it comes to your relationships?

_____

_____

_____

_____

- Are you able to forgive whoever is involved in your painful memories? Are you able to release any resentment you may be holding onto? What might you need to do to take care of your "unfinished business"?

_____

_____

_____

_____

    If you are carrying a great deal of personal pain from your past and not finding resolution for it in the present, you could probably benefit greatly from seeking the help of a trusted friend, minister, or counselor.

Taking Off Your Masks

This exercise will take about ten minutes and will help you become more aware of the masks you sometimes use to guard against feeling judged or negatively evaluated. It focuses on three areas: work, home, and church; if you'd like to add another, feel free.

I wear masks at work (or school):

Very Often   *Almost Never*

1   2   3   4   5   6   7

If your answer was between one and four, describe the kinds of masks you wear at work (or school) and with whom.

_____

_____

_____

I wear masks at home:

Very Often   *Almost Never*

1   2   3   4   5   6   7

If your answer was between one and four, describe the kinds of masks you wear at home and with whom.

_____

_____

_____

I wear masks at church:

Very Often   *Almost Never*

1   2   3   4   5   6   7

If your answer was between one and four, describe the kinds of masks you wear at church and with whom.

_____

_____

_____

    Now review your responses and determine which of your masks serves a helpful function and which ones you think may be interfering with your ability to cultivate healthy relationships. What can you do to discard these unhealthy masks?

_____

_____

Designing Your Destiny

This exercise will take about fifteen minutes or more. It is designed to help you construct a personal statement of purpose and create goals that will help you fulfill it.

To begin with, take a moment to determine what you value. It will be difficult, but force yourself to rank the following thirteen values (1 = most important to you).

_____ Achievement: Feeling satisfaction for a job well done.
_____ Challenges: Using your creativity, training, and intelligence to face challenges.
_____ Education: Increasing your intellectual understanding of life.
_____ Aesthetic Considerations: Appreciating the beauty in people, art, or nature.
_____ Health: Feeling good in a physical and emotional sense.
_____ Independence: Having freedom to do your own thing.
_____ Morality: Maintaining your moral, ethical, and religious standards.
_____ Pleasure: Having time to play and have a good time.
_____ Relationships: Caring for, sharing with, and giving to those who are close to you.
_____ Spirituality: Cultivating a meaningful and personal relationship with God.
_____ Security: Feeling safe, free from unexpected and unpleasant changes.
_____ Service to Others: Knowing you have benefited others.
_____ Wealth: Improving your financial position.

As you ponder what matters most to you, consider how your top three or four values can be incorporated into a personal purpose statement. This statement does not need to be permanent (it will change throughout your life). Just draft something that seems right for you at this time—something that is personally compelling and comes from the heart.

My purpose is . . . _____

_____

_____

Once you've drafted your purpose statement, note some specific and obtainable goals that can serve as a means to fulfill it.

Short-term goals (obtainable within the next three or four months):

1. _____

2. _____

3. _____

Long-term goals (obtainable within the next year or more):

1. _____

2. _____

3. _____

In what specific ways will you need to delay your immediate gratification in order to enjoy the benefits of meeting your goals?

_____

_____

_____

The Compulsion for Completion

The following questions are to help facilitate a meaningful small-group discussion. Feel free to explore different territory, but don't veer too far off track. In the space provided, jot down some of the group's responses to these questions. And remember, anyone is always free to "pass" on any particular question without explanation.

1. Describe your experience of completing the exercises for this chapter. What did you learn about yourself?

2. What do you make of the idea that it is only when we no longer compulsively need someone that we can ever attempt to build a healthy relationship with them? Do you agree? Why or why not?

3. Of the two lies discussed in this chapter which do you encounter more often: (1) I need this person to be complete; or (2) If this person needs me, I'll be complete?

4. How willing and comfortable are you to disclose yourself to others and let yourself be known by others? What social masks do you sometimes wear that guard you against being vulnerable? When are you most likely to wear them?

_____

_____

_____

_____

5. On a scale of one to ten, how would you rate your current tendency to delay immediate gratification? If you do this well, what's your secret? If you're striving to do this better, how can you improve?

_____

_____

_____

_____

6. It's easy to rely on another person instead of God to meet your deepest needs. Why do you think most of us struggle with this idea?

_____

_____

_____

_____

The Compulsion for Completion

To explore more of what the Bible has to say about this topic, consider the following passages:

- 1 John 4:7–21 talks about how our love for one another is predicated on God's love of us.

_____

_____

_____

- Colossians 1:19–22 talks about how God accepts us like no human can.

_____

_____

_____

- Ephesians 4:14 and 2 Corinthians 10:7 talk about our feeble attempts to find significance in surface things.

_____

_____

_____

Other books that may be of interest to you on this topic include:

- *The Search for Significance* by Robert S. McGee (Houston: Rapha, 1990).
    This book explores how we can build our self-worth on our ability to please others—or on the love and forgiveness of God. It will help you explore your goals, your motives, and your sense of identity. You will learn how to get off the performance treadmill and discover why personal success, status, beauty, and wealth do not bring lasting happiness.

- *The Road Less Traveled* by M. Scott Peck (New York: Simon and Schuster, 1977).

  On the *New York Times* best-seller's list for years, this book has become a classic for exploring personal growth issues such as delayed gratification, responsibility, emotional management, and other disciplines. Confronting and solving personal problems is a painful process that most of us try to avoid. This book may help you move beyond avoidance to actually make some changes.

- *The Marriage Builder* by Larry Crabb (Grand Rapids: Zondervan, 1992).

  Although this book is specifically for married couples, it has plenty of relevance for anyone wanting to learn more about how our deepest needs cannot be satisfied by another person, only through God (especially chapter 2).

exercises

for

chapter two

Keeping
Family Ties
from
Pulling Strings

How Healthy Is Your Home?

This exercise will take about ten minutes and will help you assess the health of your home. Understand that no family is perfect. But some families are healthier than others. In fact, Dolores Curran, in her book *Traits of a Healthy Family* (Ballantine, 1983), unveils the results of a study identifying the top fifteen traits noted again and again by family experts. They are noted below.

Using the following scale, rate the degree to which your family is characterized by these desirable traits.

4 — Much of the time
3 — Some of the time
2 — Rarely
1 — Almost never

_____ Communicates and listens
_____ Affirms and supports one another
_____ Teaches respect for others
_____ Develops a sense of trust
_____ Has a sense of play and humor
_____ Exhibits a sense of shared responsibility
_____ Teaches a sense of right and wrong
_____ Has a strong sense of family in which rituals and traditions abound
_____ Has a balance of interaction among members
_____ Has a shared religious core
_____ Respects the privacy of one another
_____ Values service to others
_____ Fosters family table time and conversation
_____ Shares leisure time
_____ Admits to and seeks help with problems
_____ Total

Scoring: Add the numbers you have placed beside each item. There is a possible total of sixty points. To interpret your score, use the following:

50–60 Count your blessings. You grew up in a relatively loving home free of dysfunction. Mom and Dad took time to nurture your development and cultivate an atmosphere that was positive and caring. Your relationships will certainly benefit from this good foundation.

30–49 Your family health falls into the midrange, or average zone. Your family may not be all you'd like it to be, but then again, things could be a lot worse. You will want to learn from the tensions and disengaged style that is sometimes present in your home. How do you contribute to it, and what can you do to make the relationships better?

1–29 This range, unfortunately, is where you will find families with the most strife. Perhaps you have experienced a lot of distressed and polarized relationships (even abusive ones) at home. If so, this will present some challenges to your present and future relationships, but nothing that can't be overcome with good relational skills.

Uncovering Unspoken Rules

This exercise will take about ten or fifteen minutes and will help you pinpoint the unspoken rules you absorbed from your family of origin.

Take your time to complete the following sentence stems. Simply complete them by writing the first thing that pops into your head:

• Men should . . . _____

_____

• Women should . . . _____

_____

• Success is . . . _____

_____

• The most important thing . . . _____

_____

• Life . . . _____

_____

Now review what you have written and edit it to conform to how you believe your parents would have completed these sentences. This will give you a pretty good start at uncovering your family's unspoken rules. Use the space below to write down any additional rules that may not have been articulated, but were still known.

_____

_____

_____

In what specific ways will your family's unspoken rules influence your relationships?

_____

Lessons Learned from Mom and Dad

We all learn by example, especially when that example is Mom and Dad. In the following relationship skill areas, note how each of your parents (or primary caretakers) behaved. You might rate their effectiveness on a scale of one to ten and then write a brief description of how each performed in that skill. This exercise will take about ten to fifteen minutes.

	Your Mother	*Your Father*
Talking about their experiences		
Showing their feelings		
Standing up for themselves		
Being a good listener		
Understanding other's perspectives		
Managing anger		
Accepting responsibility (not passing the buck)		
Working for equitable solutions		

If Your Parents Got Divorced

This exercise will take about ten minutes and will help you apply the principles discussed in the chapter.

Take a moment to list the things you have done to come to terms with your parents' divorce. In specific terms, what have you done to bring personal healing to the pain it has caused you? What things have helped the most?

_____

_____

_____

_____

How well are you managing your anger?

Not so well   *Very Well*

   1   2   3   4   5   6   7

If this is not going so well, what specific steps can you take to get it under control?

_____

_____

How well are you managing conflict-avoidance?

Not so well   *Very Well*

   1   2   3   4   5   6   7

If this is not going so well, what specific steps can you take to express your genuine feelings—even when they may cause conflict?

_____

_____

How would you rate the strength of your self-confidence?

Not so strong   *Very strong*

   1   2   3   4   5   6   7

If your self-confidence is not too strong, what specific steps can you take to build it up?

_____

_____

As you review this exercise, consider your overall health in the aftermath of your parents' divorce. If it is not getting better for you, we urge you to seek help from a competent counselor, a compassionate minister, or even a concerned friend. The strength of all your other relationships depends on it.

Keeping Family Ties
from Pulling Strings

The following questions are to help facilitate a meaningful small-group discussion. Feel free to explore different territory, but don't veer too far off track. In the space provided, jot down some of the group's responses to these questions. And remember, anyone is always free to "pass" on any particular question without explanation.

1. Describe your experience of completing the exercises for this chapter. What did you learn about yourself?

    _____

    _____

    _____

    _____

2. Can you think of another social force that has had more power in shaping your life than the family? Why or why not?

    _____

    _____

    _____

    _____

3. In what specific ways has your family of origin shaped your personality, your career choice, your relationships, your values?

    _____

    _____

    _____

    _____

4. In what specific ways does your family still "pull your strings"? In other words, how do your early family influences still manifest themselves in your present relationships?

_____

_____

_____

_____

5. Of the three major ways families shape us—rules, roles, and relationships—which one do you see as the most influential and why? Can you think of an example to underscore your reasoning?

_____

_____

_____

_____

6. If your parents are divorced, how do you think that may impact future relationships? Think of both challenges and advantages.

_____

_____

_____

_____

Keeping Family Ties
from Pulling Strings

To explore more of what the Bible has to say about this topic, consider the following passages:

- 1 Kings 22 is just one biblical example of how powerful the family's impact is.

_____

_____

_____

- Ephesians 5:21–33 talks about the relationship of husbands and wives, the architects of every family.

_____

_____

_____

- Romans 8:28 gives encouraging words for everyone who has not had the greatest home life.

_____

_____

_____

Other books that may be of interest to you on this topic include:

- *Intimate Worlds: Life Inside the Family* by Maggie Scarf (New York: Random House, 1995).

    This is a serious examination of the complexities of families. The author combines clear analysis with meaningful stories to expose the core issues that every family must deal with.

- *The Tribute* by Dennis Rainey and David Boehi (Nashville: Thomas Nelson, 1994).

    If you are looking for ways to develop a more meaningful relationship with your parents, this book can serve as your guide to resolving issues from the past and blessing your parents in the present.

- *Family Shock* by Gary R. Collins (Wheaton: Tyndale, 1995).

    This book is filled with expert analysis, true stories, and practical advice on keeping families strong in the midst of earthshaking change. This one doesn't shy away from tough topics, and it imparts an uplifting and optimistic message about families.

exercises

for

chapter three

Crossing
the
Gender Line

What's Your Gender I.Q.?

This exercise will take about five minutes and will help you get a general idea of how much you already know about some fundamental differences between the genders. Answer each of the following items as either true or false.

1. T F Women are better spellers than men.

2. T F Men are more likely than women to use conversation to solve problems.

3. T F Women have larger connections between their brain's left and right hemispheres.

4. T F Men are better at reading the emotions of others than women are.

5. T F Men score higher on the math section of the SAT than do women.

6. T F In comparison to men, women are better at maintaining a sense of geographical direction.

7. T F Men are better than women at fitting suitcases into a crowded car trunk.

8. T F Women are better than men at describing their feelings.

9. T F Men, more than women, focus their energy on achievement.

10. T F Women, more than men, give priority to relationships.

Scoring: Each of these items is based on current gender research studies. Note how many of the items you got correct. 1-T, 2-T, 3-T, 4-F, 5-T, 6-F, 7-T, 8-T, 9-T, 10-T. The higher your score, the better your base knowledge of gender differences.

What If You
Were the Opposite Sex?

This exercise can take as little as fifteen minutes to much longer. As strange and as difficult as this might seem, do your best to imagine what it would be like to live as the opposite sex. In other words, if you are a man, what would life be like for you if you were a woman? And if you are a woman, what would it be like to live as a man? With this in mind, answer the following questions as honestly as you can.

1. What is your first reaction to living as the opposite sex?

_____

_____

_____

2. How would the simple task of getting ready in the morning be different if you were the opposite gender (e.g., the time it would take, what you would do, how you would dress)?

_____

_____

_____

3. How would living as the opposite sex affect your career choice and other aspirations?

_____

_____

_____

4. As the opposite gender, would you feel more or less safe in society? Why?

_____

_____

_____

5. Would you feel any different about dating and the prospect of marriage if you were the opposite gender? If so, how?

_____

_____

_____

6. How would your relationship with both your mom and dad differ if you were the opposite gender?

_____

_____

_____

Once you have taken the time to answer these questions, you may find it insightful to share your answers with another person who has completed the same exercise.

A Self-Test for Women Only

This exercise will take about ten minutes and will help you review and apply some important insights in understanding the men in your life. Take a moment to reflect on what the book has to say about "what women need to know about men." For each of the statements below, note an example from your own life that illustrates the point.

Men are not as in touch with their emotions as we are.

_____

_____

_____

Men are more independent than we are.

_____

_____

_____

Men are more abstract than we are.

_____

_____

_____

Next, consider what you can do in practical terms to bridge the gender gap with the most important men in your life. In other words, how can you apply the above insights to these relationships?

_____

_____

_____

_____

_____

_____

exercise twelve

A Self-Test for Men Only

This exercise will take about ten minutes and will help you review and apply some important insights in understanding the women in your life. Take a moment to reflect on what the book has to say about "what men need to know about women." For each of the statements below, note an example from your own life that illustrates the point.

Women are not as independent as we are.

_____

_____

_____

Women focus on the here-and-now more than we do.

_____

_____

_____

Women are not as competitive as we are.

_____

_____

_____

Next, consider what you can do in practical terms to bridge the gender gap with the most important women in your life. In other words, how can you apply the above insights to these relationships?

_____

_____

_____

_____

_____

group discussion
on chapter three

Crossing the Gender Line

The following questions are to help facilitate a meaningful small-group discussion. Feel free to explore different territory, but don't veer too far off track. In the space provided, jot down some of the group's responses to these questions. And remember, anyone is always free to "pass" on any particular question without explanation.

1. Describe your experience of completing the exercises for this chapter. What did you learn about yourself?

_____

_____

_____

_____

2. Consider your cross-gender relationships. What aspects of these relationships with the opposite sex (excluding romantic relationships) seem to be easier than relationships with the same sex? What are the biggest hurdles you encounter in relating with the opposite sex?

_____

_____

_____

_____

3. When you were growing up as a kid, what social activities or games do you think influenced your gender roles? Looking back on it, do you put more stock in the way your environment shaped you or the way your biology programmed you?

_____

_____

_____

_____

4. This chapter notes several things men and women should know about the opposite gender. What differences could you add?

_____

_____

_____

_____

5. Have you noticed how women use their conversation to build "rapport" while men use conversation to give or get the "report"? What examples of this disparity can you remember from your own experience?

_____

_____

_____

_____

6. The major point of this chapter is that we doom our relationships with the opposite sex when we try to change them into being more like us. If this is so, what can you do to accept and even appreciate the different qualities of the other gender?

_____

_____

_____

_____

Crossing the Gender Line

To explore more of what the Bible has to say about this topic, consider the following passages:

- Genesis 1:27 talks of both male and female being created in the image of God.

_____

_____

_____

- Galatians 3:28 instructs us in the equality and unity of the genders before God in Christ.

_____

_____

_____

- Ephesians 4:4–8 reminds us that although we each have been given different gifts, we are one in Christ.

_____

_____

_____

Other books that may be of interest to you on this topic include:

- Men & Women: Enjoying the Difference by Larry Crabb (Grand Rapids: Zondervan, 1991).

    According to psychologist Larry Crabb, men and women share a deadly problem that kills good relating. The problem is this: we are committed, first of all, to ourselves. Each of us, without blushing, holds fast to an overriding concern for our own well-being. Giving numerous examples from his counseling office, Crabb explores how we can turn away from ourselves and toward each other, how we can become what he calls "other-centered."

- *Men Are from Mars, Women Are from Venus* by John Gray (New York: HarperCollins, 1992).

    Using his now famous metaphor to illustrate the commonly occurring conflicts between men and women, John Gray explains how gender differences can come between the sexes and prohibit mutually fulfilling loving relationships. He gives advice on how to counteract these differences in communication styles, emotional needs, and modes of behavior to promote a greater understanding between individuals.

- *Can Men and Women Be Just Friends?* by Andy Bustanoby (Grand Rapids: Zondervan, 1993).

    This helpful book helps both men and women understand what friendship is and how to handle opposite-sex friendships. Bustanoby explains that friendships between the opposite sex are possible with certain boundaries, and he carefully outlines these boundaries in the book.

exercises

for

chapter four

Friends
to Die For

The Friendship Assessment

This exercise will help you evaluate the current condition of each of your friendships. It will take about ten minutes or so, depending on how many friendships you evaluate.

Have a specific friend in mind and then answer each of the following true and false questions as honestly as you can.

T   F   This person knows how to keep a secret.

T   F   We can disagree and then make up without holding grudges.

T   F   This person almost always makes time for me, and I do the same for him/her.

T   F   When he/she gives me advice, it is generally without judgment.

T   F   I can totally be myself around this person.

T   F   He/she is a good listener.

T   F   This person has stuck by me through tough times and is willing to make personal sacrifices for me.

T   F   This person knows my faults, but loves me anyway.

T   F   Our relationship is balanced with give and take; we are equally vulnerable and caring.

T   F   I am able to set clear boundaries with this person when necessary and he/she respects them.

T   F   No subject is off-limits in our conversation.

T   F   I can always count on this person.

_____ Total number of "T" responses for . . .

_____ Total number of "T" responses for . . .

_____ Total number of "T" responses for . . .

_____ Total number of "T" responses for . . .

Scoring: Add up the number of true responses you have for each friendship you evaluated. There is a possible total of twelve points for each relationship. To interpret your score, use the following:

10–12 No doubt about it, this is a good friend who is worth all the effort, care, and investment. You will want to do all that you can to nurture this relationship and enjoy it.

7–9 Although this person could be more sensitive to your needs, this amigo shows great potential. Be careful, however, not to set yourself up for disappointment if this person doesn't meet all your expectations.

0–6 This friend is probably too fair-weather to see you through stormy times (and maybe even the sunny ones, too). Don't hang all your hopes on this one.

Are You a "Growth Promoting" Listener?

Most of us have a lot of room for improvement when it comes to learning to listen. This exercise will help you assess your strengths and areas for growth when it comes to this important friendship skill. It will take about five or ten minutes.

It is important that you be honest in answering each of the following three items. Each one asks you about one of the primary aspects of what Carl Rogers called "growth promoting" listening. Simply circle the number that most accurately indicates where you would be on the continuums.

Generally speaking, in meeting someone for the first time at a party, are you *genuinely* interested in getting to know them and understanding their story? Do you really want to know what interests them? Or are you more likely to just go through the motions, being socially appropriate but not very genuine?

Not Genuine   *Extremely Genuine*

  1   2   3   4   5   6   7

Generally speaking, in meeting someone for the first time at a party, are you *accepting* of that person's opinions and feelings? Do you feel open to hearing what they have to say, or are you more likely to interject your opinions and feelings before completely understanding theirs?

Not Accepting   *Extremely Accepting*

  1   2   3   4   5   6   7

Generally speaking, in meeting someone for the first time at a party, are you *empathic* with them? Do you put yourself in their shoes and try to accurately understand their experience, or are you more likely to jump to a few conclusions and make a few assumptions?

Not Empathic   *Extremely Empathic*

  1   2   3   4   5   6   7

____   Total Score

Scoring and Interpretation: Add up the numbers you have circled. There is a total of twenty-one points possible and the higher your score, the more likely you are to be a "growth promoting" listener. However, you may find it most helpful to consider each continuum separately to see which of the three important qualities you will want to work on most.

Are You a Fair-weather Friend?

This exercise will take about five minutes and will help you assess how loyal you are to your friends. Consider what your friends would say about you when it comes to the following statements. Answer yes or no to each of these items and be as honest as you can.

My friends would say . . .

Y N I always keep my promises.

Y N I always stick up for them.

Y N I give them grace when they let me down.

Y N I am just as likely to genuinely celebrate my friends' successes as I am to comfort them in their disappointments.

Y N I am there when they need me.

Y N I am ready and willing to lend them a hand.

Y N I never gossip about them or talk behind their back.

Y N I give them the benefit of the doubt.

Y N I hear them out even when I disagree.

Y N I stand by them through thick and thin.

Scoring: The more items you honestly responded to with a yes, the more likely you are to be loyal to your friends. If you answered yes to nearly all of the items, however, you probably shouldn't take this quality in yourself for granted. Check in with your pals. Ask them to give you a loyalty checkup by inviting them for honest feedback on how you are doing with being loyal. On the other hand, if you did not answer yes to very many of these items, you may want to talk to your friends about how you can better cultivate this quality. Remember, loyalty is what tops the list of what people appreciate most about their friends, so this is one you will want to spend some time on.

Determining
Your Dedication Quotient

How dedicated are you to your friends? This exercise will help you answer this question. It will take as little as ten minutes to much longer, depending on whether you discuss your answers with another person who has done the same exercise.

Consider your closest friendships and think about them as you put yourself in the following scenarios. Indicate how you would respond, and feel free to write your own response to better capture what you would say.

Scenario One

You get a call from one of your good friends at 2:00 A.M. He recently called it quits with someone he has been dating for several months, and now he is having second thoughts.

Do you say . . .

    a. "I can't believe you're calling me at 2:00 A.M. I've got to sleep."

    b. "I am so sorry, but I can't even think clearly at this hour. Let's meet over breakfast."

    c. "Tell me how you're doing."

    d. Other: _____

Scenario Two

One of your good friends is moving to a new apartment on Saturday and asks you to help out by lending a hand and also loaning her your car. You have an important project due on Monday and you were planning on using your weekend to do it. You're also not that crazy about using your car as a moving van.

Do you say . . .

    a. "I'd love to help you, but there is just no possible way."

    b. "I can help you for a couple of hours in the morning, but I've got to work on my project in the afternoon."

c. "No problem. Whatever it takes to help a friend."

d. Other: _____

Scenario Three

One of your good friends shows interest in dating someone you had once dated seriously (for about six months). You currently have no attachments to this person, but you have uneasy feelings about the two of them getting together. Your friend asks you how you feel about it.

Do you say . . .

a. "If you go out, I don't see how we can still be friends."

b. "Sure, I don't mind." (And secretly resent it.)

c. "To be honest, I have funny feelings about it, but I'm not sure why."

d. Other: _____

The point of this exercise is to get you thinking about your level of dedication to your friendships. None of the answers is the only "right" one; there is no objective score to be obtained. You may, however, find it helpful to compare your responses with someone else to get some objective feedback. Ask each other why you chose the answers you did and whether you feel good about them. Consider whether you are more dedicated in certain areas (e.g., during times of immediate crisis) than you are in others. And why you are more dedicated to some friends than you are to others. Finally, if you are feeling like your dedication level is lacking, explore concrete ways you can improve it.

Friends to Die For

The following questions are to help facilitate a meaningful small-group discussion. Feel free to explore different territory, but don't veer too far off track. In the space provided, jot down some of the group's responses to these questions. And remember, anyone is always free to "pass" on any particular question without explanation.

1. Describe your experience of completing the exercises for this chapter. What did you learn about yourself?

_____

_____

_____

_____

2. It has been said that many people audition to be our friends but only a few make the cut. What is it about your friends that caused them to get the part? Did it have more to do with circumstances or personal qualities?

_____

_____

_____

_____

3. The medical benefits of having friends is quite remarkable. What benefits of the less scientific kind do you appreciate? What fruits of friendship do you enjoy the most?

_____

_____

_____

_____

4. Do you agree that generally speaking, our good friends come in two forms: as friends of the road and friends of the heart? Think of an example of a meaningful friendship that did not last. What purpose did it serve in your life or what passage did it see you through?

_____

_____

_____

_____

5. Forgiveness can be one of the most challenging struggles for any relationship. Think of a time when you were either on the receiving or the giving end of forgiveness. What makes it so difficult?

_____

_____

_____

_____

6. Of the four qualities that keep friendships going—loyalty, forgiveness, honesty, and dedication—which one is most important to you and why? What other qualities would you add to this list?

_____

_____

_____

_____

Friends to Die For

To explore more of what the Bible has to say about this topic, consider the following passages:

• Ruth 1:1–18 talks about a woman who went far beyond what was expected for a friend.

_____

_____

_____

• Job 2:1–13 talks about how true friendship offers comfort when the pain is beyond understanding.

_____

_____

_____

• 2 Timothy 1:1–18 talks about the importance of encouragement in strengthening friendship.

_____

_____

_____

Other books that may be of interest to you on this topic include:

• *Just Friends: The Role of Friendship in Our Lives* by Lillian B. Rubin (New York: Harper & Row, 1985).

Drawing on years of study, Rubin covers the full range of friendships and their interrelations with kinship, marriage, and romance. She exposes the ambiguity, ambivalence, and contradiction with which friendship in our society is hedged.

- *Making Real Friends in a Phony World* by Jim Conway (Grand Rapids: Zondervan, 1989).

    If you're tired of surface relationships and want to achieve new depth in your relationships with family, coworkers, and fellow Christians, this book will show you what it takes to make—and be—a real friend.

- *The Four Loves* by C. S. Lewis (New York: Harcourt Brace Jovanovich, 1960).

    In this classic book, C. S. Lewis provides a candid, wise, and warmly personal look at four basic kinds of human love—affection, friendship, erotic love, and the love of God. Lewis, among other things, explores the possibilities and problems of friendships between men and women. He reveals the virtues and failings of this human longing, and he also explores the questions of sex, possessiveness, jealousy, pride, and false sentimentality.

exercises

for

chapter five

What to Do
When
Friends Fail

What You Expect from Friends

This exercise will take about five minutes and will help you clarify what you expect from your closest friends. Answer the following true-and-false items as honestly as you can.

T F   I expect my friend to know my faults but accept me anyway.

T F   I expect my friend to never break special plans with me—even for a date at the last minute.

T F   I expect my close friends to always keep their word on both big and small issues.

T F   A really good friend should know how I'm feeling most of the time.

T F   I expect my friend to say "I'm sorry" when he or she is wrong.

T F   My closest friend should confide in me more than anyone else.

T F   I expect my friend to always keep a secret.

T F   It is difficult for me to forgive a friend who has hurt me in some way.

T F   If we are truly friends, we should hardly ever have much conflict.

T F   I expect my friends to never talk behind my back or break a confidence—even about small things.

T F   My very closest friend should have no other friendships closer than ours.

T F   If a good friend breaks a confidence or fails me in some other way, I am unlikely to give him or her a second or third chance.

T F   I expect my friend to never hold a grudge against me.

T F   I expect my friend to always admit when he or she is wrong.

If you answered true to any of these items, you are more likely to have very high standards about how your friends should treat you. The more times you answered true, the more you expect from your friends and perhaps the more rigid you are with your expectations.

Learning from
Your Own Failed Friendships

This exercise can take as little as ten minutes. It is designed to help you gain insight into how you can avoid repeating patterns of painful relationships. Take your time as you consider a relationship where a person you trusted failed you in some way, and answer the following questions to help you learn from the failure.

• How long did you know this person, and what brought you together?

_____

• Looking back over your relationship, what kinds of things helped you to believe you could trust him or her?

_____

_____

• In specific terms, what did this person do to "fail" you?

_____

_____

• What percentage of the hurt was due to the following:

Percentage

____ miscommunication
____ broken confidence
____ gossip
____ neglect
____ betrayal
____ uncontrollable change (moving)
____ personality change
____ moral choices
____ other _____

- Take a moment for some serious soul searching and try to assess how much you were responsible for the falling out with this friend. Was there anything you did or didn't do that may have contributed to the problem? If so, what was it?

_____

_____

- Did you ever want to get revenge as a result of the hurt you felt from this relationship, and if so, why? Also, what did you do with your vengeful feelings and what was the result?

_____

_____

- Have you come to a place of healing with the hurt you experienced? If so, what helped bring this about?

_____

_____

- In reviewing the basis for your relationship and the reasons for your fallout, what can you surmise about how to avoid a similar situation in future friendships?

_____

_____

Can This Friendship Be Saved?

This exercise will take about five to ten minutes and is designed to help you assess the status of an increasingly troublesome friendship. Consider your particular relationship and take a moment to answer yes or no to the following questions.

Y N You find that one of you is always saying, after the other says hello, "Sorry I didn't get back to you, I've been so busy."

Y N You've made a date with a friend and later schedule another appointment at the same time without realizing it.

Y N You find you talk more about your friend to others than you do to your friend.

Y N When you get together with your friend, you find yourself sitting silently, refusing to ask how she is, and you realize that you're waiting for her to first ask you how you are; it doesn't happen.

Y N You don't like yourself after you've been with him, because he can bring out the worst in you.

Y N You realize that you no longer feel safe being completely honest with her about your personal life.

Y N You're losing patience with his chronic lateness and are frequently mumbling "I've had it" under your breath.

Y N You've reminisced about the past for the fifth straight time and realize that there's an increasing lack of current history between you.

Y N You've talked to your friend about how you feel hurt or neglected and yet there are no signs of positive change.

Y N You feel forced by the relationship to compromise your principles or subvert your self-respect.

____ Number of yes responses

If you circled yes on three or more of the above statements, your friendship needs work. But unfortunately, it might be beyond repair. Some betrayals are just too big to forgive and forget. Some friendships are so flawed they constantly weigh you down. Other times friends simply outgrow each other. While no one but you can make the decision whether or not to end a friendship, if you've circled yes on most of the above items, you shouldn't ignore the option.

Making Amends

This exercise can take as much as fifteen minutes or longer. While it may appear to be somewhat rigid or systematic, please do not let it keep you from doing whatever your heart is telling you to do to make amends with the person you care about. Consider these steps as guidelines to help you bring healing and restoration to a floundering friendship.

Step One: Count the Cost

What is the price you are paying to keep this friendship alive? If you were forced to choose between the following two statements, which one would best describe how you feel about this friendship?

1. This friendship has redeeming qualities I value and is worth the cost of repairing and maintaining.

2. This friendship is unhealthy and forces me to compromise my convictions.

If you chose the second statement, it is time to make a clean break. If you chose the first statement, you are ready to make amends by progressing to the next step.

Step Two: Make Meaningful Contact

You now need to determine the best way to convey the following message to your friend: "Our friendship is valuable to me, and I miss seeing you. Is there any way we can resolve what stands between us?" Knowing your friend as you do, would it be best to convey this message in writing (with a brief note), on the phone, or in person? Once you determine the means, take care to send the right message by cleaning your heart and mind of lingering desires to get back at your friend. Take a moment right now to note what has hurt you and how you may still want to get even. Be honest with yourself about your anger and feelings of revenge.

_____

_____

_____

_____

Step Three: Forgive as Best You Can

Once you have a handle on your hurt and angry feelings, you will need to do your best to step beyond them by trying to forgive. This is not an easy step, but it is vital to making amends. It begins by putting yourself in your friend's shoes and seeing the relationship and situation from his or her perspective.

- How do you imagine your friend feels about what is going on between the two of you?

_____

_____

- Is your friend feeling as hurt as you are? If so, why?

_____

_____

- If the roles were reversed, how do you think the relationship would be different?

_____

_____

- Knowing that hardly any relationship problem is ever entirely one person's fault, what do you take responsibility for in this situation?

_____

_____

- Are you able and willing to set aside your pride and give grace to your friend? If so, how can you do this?

_____

_____

Step Four: Diagnose the Problem

Once you have come to a place where you can forgive your friend and convey the simple message of wanting to make things right, the two of you may need to explore together why the problem emerged so that it won't happen again. It's up to the two of you to determine whether this step of having an honest discussion of differences is necessary.

Step Five: Rebuild Respect

This last step is critical to making amends. Ask yourself what traits your friend possesses that inspire you to become a better person and then make a list of a half dozen of your friend's most admirable qualities.

1. _____

2. _____

3. _____

4. _____

5. _____

6. _____

Now that you have made this list, you are ready to offer a sincere apology to your friend and express to him or her just how important the relationship is to you and how much you appreciate his or her qualities.

What to Do When Friends Fail

The following questions are to help facilitate a meaningful small-group discussion. Feel free to explore different territory, but don't veer too far off track. In the space provided, jot down some of the group's responses to these questions. And remember, anyone is always free to "pass" on any particular question without explanation.

1. Describe your experience of completing the exercises for this chapter. What did you learn about yourself?

_____

_____

_____

_____

2. As you consider particular friendships you have lost along the way, are there some that are more important to you than others? If so, why? What makes them valuable to you, and how do you feel about rebuilding a connection with them?

_____

_____

_____

_____

3. What do you think about the idea that what we expect from our friendships will determine whether or not those friendships can hold up under turbulent times? Think of some examples of expectations of a friend that cross the line. How do you determine that?

_____

_____

_____

_____

4. The chapter points out that most friendships fail because of one of three things: positive or negative change in one person's life, neglect of the relationship, or blatant betrayal that is either intentional or unintentional. As you consider your own failed friendships, what can the cause tell you about finding a "cure"?

_____

_____

_____

_____

5. How can you personally determine whether a broken relationship should be repaired or not? In other words, how do you decide if your differences are truly irreconcilable or not?

_____

_____

_____

_____

6. When it comes to the practical side of mending a broken relationship with a friend, which of the five steps suggested in this chapter (count the cost, make contact, forgive, diagnose the problem, and rebuild respect) would be most difficult for you to take and why? What could you do to make taking this step a bit easier?

_____

_____

_____

_____

What to Do When Friends Fail

To explore more of what the Bible has to say about this topic consider the following passages:

- Psalm 55:12–14 and 20–21 describe David's shock over a betrayal by his close friend.

_____

_____

_____

- Galatians 6:1–5 talks about bearing with the failures of our friends.

_____

_____

_____

- The short book of Philemon encourages reconciliation of friendship after experiencing a difficult conflict.

_____

_____

_____

Other books that may be of interest to you on this topic include:

- *High-Maintenance Relationships* by Les Parrott (Wheaton: Tyndale, 1996).
  Whether they be Control Freaks, Backstabbers, Gossips, Chameleons, Volcanos, Flirts, Martyrs, or Critics, here you will find practical suggestions and advice to help you understand and cope with difficult friendships. Take the self-test in the first chapter to pinpoint what kind of relationship you are dealing with and then find dozens of practical suggestions for making immediate improvements.

- *Safe People* by Henry Cloud and John Townsend (Grand Rapids: Zondervan, 1995).

    If you are wondering why you sometimes choose the wrong people to be your friends, this book will offer an explanation. It will also help you learn about things within yourself that jeopardize your relational security. On a very practical level, Cloud and Townsend will offer solid guidance for making safe choices in relationships by helping you identify nurturing people. This is a book of encouragement and hope.

- *Hope When You're Hurting* by Larry Crabb and Dan Allender (Grand Rapids: Zondervan, 1996).

    Where do you turn when a friend has let you down? Do you go to a counselor? Drs. Crabb and Allender point the way as they pose four key questions hurting people need to ask: What's wrong? Who can help? What will the helper do? and What can I hope for? This book will provide guidance, choices, and hope for dealing with the pain of a friend who has failed you.

exercises

for

chapter six

Falling in Love Without Losing Your Mind

What's Your Love I.Q.?

This exercise will take about five or ten minutes. If you honestly answer the following items, you will have a clearer understanding of your "love smarts."

Would you say that you choose love or that love chooses you?

Love Chooses Me   *I Choose Love*

1   2   3   4   5   6   7

Are you likely to date almost anyone rather than to go without a date at all?

Almost Anyone   *Go Without*

1   2   3   4   5   6   7

Do you have a clear understanding of what qualities and character traits you want in the person you date, or are you more likely to discover that along the way?

Discover It Along the Way   *Know What I Want*

1   2   3   4   5   6   7

Do you tend to make decisions based more on the way you feel or on the way you think?

Feeling   *Thinking*

1   2   3   4   5   6   7

If a person you are physically attracted to holds values and convictions that blatantly conflict with yours, are you more likely to explore the dating relationship or move on?

Explore   *Move On*

1   2   3   4   5   6   7

If you really like the person, but after a few dates he or she show signs of disrespecting you, are you able to see what's going on and let that person know it, or are you more likely to keep quiet and put up with it?

Keep Quiet and Put Up With It   *See It and Talk About It*

1   2   3   4   5   6   7

When it comes to physical passion, are you able to set your own boundaries and stay under control, or are you more likely to let your date call all the shots?

Let My Date Set the Speed   *Set Boundaries and Keep Them*

   1   2   3   4   5   6   7

Do you believe in love at first sight or slowly simmering love?

First-sight Love   *Slow-growth Love*

   1   2   3   4   5   6   7

Scoring Procedure: tally your score to determine where you rank on the following level:

37–56   Above Average Love I.Q.

25–36   Average Love I.Q.

7–24   Below Average Love I.Q.

The point of this exercise is to help you assess your natural present inklings when it comes to dating relationships. Don't be discouraged by your score if it falls below average. This simply means that you may have more to gain from the principles discussed in this chapter of the book.

Are You a Good Match?

This exercise can take about five minutes and will help you determine whether the person you are dating possesses qualities and characteristics that fit the bill for you in the long run.

For each of the items in the following list, make a check mark for those qualities, traits, skills, or characteristics you possess in common with your dating partner.

Things We Have in Common

- ❑ Age
- ❑ Dependability
- ❑ Sense of humor
- ❑ Sincerity
- ❑ Religious convictions
- ❑ Family backgrounds
- ❑ Ability to adjust to things beyond your control
- ❑ Level of education
- ❑ Roles of women and men
- ❑ Political views
- ❑ Patience
- ❑ Use of alcohol and drugs
- ❑ Preference in music and entertainment
- ❑ Expression of emotions
- ❑ Management of anger
- ❑ Hobbies and activities
- ❑ Attitudes toward money
- ❑ Generosity
- ❑ Social skills
- ❑ Humility
- ❑ Hygiene standards

❑ Optimism
❑ Self-discipline and self-control

There is no numeric score for this exercise. The checklist is simply a tool for helping you see how much or how little you have in common with a person you are dating.

exercise twenty-three

The True You Self-Test

This exercise will take about five minutes and will help you assess whether you are more likely to determine for yourself who you will be or whether you are more likely to be influenced by outside forces. Indicate your level of agreement for each of the following items.

1. I often feel helpless in dealing with the problems of life.

   ❑ Strongly Agree   ❑ Agree   ❑ Disagree   ❑ Strongly Disagree

2. What happens to me in the future mostly depends on me.

   ❑ Strongly Agree   ❑ Agree   ❑ Disagree   ❑ Strongly Disagree

3. I have little control over the things that happen to me.

   ❑ Strongly Agree   ❑ Agree   ❑ Disagree   ❑ Strongly Disagree

4. There is really no way I can solve some of the problems I have.

   ❑ Strongly Agree   ❑ Agree   ❑ Disagree   ❑ Strongly Disagree

5. I can do just about anything I really set my mind to.

   ❑ Strongly Agree   ❑ Agree   ❑ Disagree   ❑ Strongly Disagree

6. Sometimes I feel that I'm being pushed around in life.

   ❑ Strongly Agree   ❑ Agree   ❑ Disagree   ❑ Strongly Disagree

7. There is little I can do to change many of the important things in my life.

   ❑ Strongly Agree   ❑ Agree   ❑ Disagree   ❑ Strongly Disagree

The preceding items are designed to measure how much you have a sense of mastery and control over your life. Agreement with items 2 and 5 and disagreement with the remaining items indicate that you have what psychologists call an "internal locus of control"—that is, the belief that you are in control of and responsible for what happens in your life. Disagreement with items 2 and 5 and agreement with the remaining items indicate an "external locus of control"—the belief that what happens to you is determined by chance and that you are not responsible. These items cannot be considered the definitive test of your locus of control, but they can help you think about your own sense of taking responsibility and being true to yourself.

While the desire to be something or someone you are not may be tempting when trying to woo someone, it almost always spells disaster. For this reason, a stronger internal locus means you are more likely to be true to yourself.

Determining Your Bottom Line

This exercise will take about ten minutes and will help you uncover what you will and will not live with in a dating relationship. Take a moment to respond to each of the following questions. And remember, everyone's bottom line is different. So don't answer for anyone else but yourself.

When it comes to common courtesy from your dating partner, what do you expect?

_____

_____

_____

When it comes to seeing other people during different stages of a dating relationship, where do you draw the line?

_____

_____

_____

When it comes to expressing physical intimacy, where do you draw the line?

_____

_____

_____

When it comes to personal values, religious beliefs, and spirituality, where do you draw the line?

_____

_____

_____

Falling in Love Without Losing Your Mind

The following questions are to help facilitate a meaningful small-group discussion. Feel free to explore different territory, but don't veer too far off track. In the space provided, jot down some of the group's responses to these questions. And remember, anyone is always free to "pass" on any particular question without explanation.

1. Describe your experience of completing the exercises for this chapter. What did you learn about yourself?

_____

_____

_____

_____

2. In specific terms, how would you describe the emotions surrounding infatuation and falling in love? Are they the same thing?

_____

_____

_____

_____

3. Journalist Helen Rowland said, "Falling in love consists merely in uncorking the imagination and bottling the common sense." In what ways does falling in love impair our judgment and deplete our common sense?

_____

_____

_____

_____

4. Do you agree that detecting your partner's values can be one of the smartest moves you make while dating? Why or why not? If you believe it is important, how do you go about discovering them?

_____

_____

_____

_____

5. How have you tried to change another person to please you more? And how have you tried to change yourself to please another person? In both cases, what was the result?

_____

_____

_____

_____

6. What "bottom lines" have you determined for yourself in dating other people? Do you need to communicate them to the person you are dating? If so, how do you do this?

_____

_____

_____

_____

Falling in Love
Without Losing Your Mind

To explore more of what the Bible has to say about this topic, consider the following passages:

• Genesis 29:18 tells the story of Jacob falling in love with Rachel.

_____

_____

_____

_____

• Judges 16 shows the serious consequences of Samson losing his mind as he falls in love with Delilah.

_____

_____

_____

_____

• Song of Solomon 8:6–7 talks about the powerful experience of being in love.

_____

_____

_____

_____

Other books that may be of interest to you on this topic include:

• *Finding the Love of Your Life* by Neil Clark Warren (Colorado Springs: Focus on the Family, 1992).

This book provides proven principles to help you choose the right person to marry. More specifically, it will show you how to eliminate the seven most prevalent causes of faulty mate selection, how to develop a clear mental image of your spouse, how to let passionate love mature before you decide to marry, how to clear conflict from the road of love, and how to celebrate your marriage with the full support of family and friends.

- *Keeping the Love You Find* by Harville Hendrix (New York: Pocket Books, 1992).

  Even the most well-adjusted people can have unresolved conflicts that make them seek out unsuitable romantic partners, unwittingly sabotage their relationships, and run from commitment without ever knowing why. This book will help you to start off your next relationship in a healthful manner and keep you loving for a lifetime.

exercises
for
chapter seven

Sex, Lies, and the Great Escape

Your Most Important Sex Organ

This exercise can take as little as five minutes. But take your time to give serious consideration to the questions it poses.

Most people who "lose control" in the heat of the moment blame it on their hormones. "There's nothing I could have done to restrain myself," they say. What do you think? On the following scale rate how much control you think we human beings have over our sexual activity.

Total Control   *No Control*

| 1 | 2 | 3 | 4 | 5 | 6 | 7 | 8 | 9 | 10 |

If you circled 2 or higher, how do you explain your answer? Do you really believe that in a romantic relationship there comes a point where a couple simply can no longer control their physical attraction? That it is beyond their capacity to sexually restrain themselves? If you believe this, how do you substantiate your position?

_____

_____

_____

_____

Experts agree that human beings do have the capacity to be in total control of their sexual urges. Thanks to the cortex of our brain, we are different from animals. We can make decisions that govern how we will behave. With this in mind, consider what you can do personally to turn on your brain power when you are faced with a strong temptation to give in to sexual urges. Be as specific and as practical as possible.

_____

_____

_____

_____

If you are comfortable sharing your ideas with another person, compare them with someone of the same gender.

The Bonds That Bind

This exercise will take about ten minutes. Emotional bonding—if it is to be healthy and long lasting—systematically progresses through some predictable stages. Research has revealed that the reason many relationships don't last is because the foundation for bonding is too often short-circuited. Take a moment to examine the following stages of physical intimacy:

1. Eye to body
2. Eye to eye
3. Voice to voice
4. Hand to hand
5. Hand to shoulder
6. Hand to waist
7. Face to face
8. Hand to head
9. Hand to body
10. Mouth to breast
11. Touching below the waist
12. Intercourse

As you review this progression of physical bonding, make note of how far your most intimate relationships have gone and how long it took you to get there. What were the consequences? You probably don't want to write down such personal information in this workbook, but you may want to jot down a few general thoughts on how moving prematurely through any of these stages may result in unhealthy consequences for a relationship. You might consider using a metaphor in articulating your thoughts (e.g., skipping a stage is like leaving a brick out of a foundation).

_____

_____

_____

Ideally, how quickly (or slowly) do you personally think couples should progress through each stage? Make some notes next to each of the above stages.

Do you have some thoughts on what might happen in any of these particular stages if they are experienced too quickly or even skipped altogether?

_____

_____

_____

Drawing the Line

This exercise will take about ten minutes and will help you answer some of the most important relationship questions you will ever ask. Where do you draw the line? Do you only kiss before getting married? Do you do anything as long as you both keep your pants on? What have you decided is right for you, and how do you stick to your decision? To help you explore and set boundaries in your intimate relationships, review the physical intimacy scale you read about in the book:

The Physical Intimacy Scale

1. Embracing and hand holding
2. Cuddling and gentle caressing
3. Polite kissing on the lips
4. Passionate total mouth kissing
5. Intense and prolonged total mouth kissing
6. Fondling breasts and genitals outside the clothes
7. Fondling breasts and genitals under the clothes
8. Oral or genital stimulation to orgasm outside the clothes
9. Oral or genital stimulation to orgasm under the clothes
10. Genital intercourse

Again, you may not want to write this information here, but think about these questions. Where do you draw the line? Why?

_____

_____

_____

_____

What are the consequences of where you draw the line for you and your relationship (e.g., do you risk shutting off your sexuality completely; are you playing with fire; are you making intercourse inevitable)?

_____

_____

Once you have given this some thought and made a careful decision, consider what you will need to do to keep from crossing that line. This is a critically important step—and couples will get into trouble if it is not taken. So what practical things can you do to be sure you stick to your decision? What behaviors and what places do you need to avoid? What can you do in place of the risky behaviors? Consider a variety of scenarios and be as specific as possible.

Healing the Hurt of Sexual Regret

This exercise will take fifteen minutes or longer and is designed exclusively for readers who have made unhealthy sexual decisions and need to recover from the consequences. This may be a difficult exercise, but it is crucial to helping you find healing and getting a fresh start.

First, you need to recount in specific terms exactly what pain and hurt you carry with you from having sex-too-soon. What troubles you most about your experience? If you don't want to write in this book, find another place where you can record your feelings.

_____

_____

_____

Once you have identified your heartache, you will need to take several steps to find your freedom from regret and pain. One of the best action plans we know of is found in Dick Purnell's book *Free to Love Again* (Thomas Nelson, 1989). Here are the steps he recommends:

1. Accept God's forgiveness.
2. Forgive yourself.
3. Expect powerful changes.
4. Guard your mind.
5. Dissolve immoral relationships.
6. Purify your passions.
7. Focus your future.

From the above list, which steps would seem to trip you up most and why?

_____

_____

_____

Of course, a brief exercise in a workbook is not going to restore your spirit and erase your sexual regrets. This is only a start. Healing is always a process that takes time. So give yourself permission to be patient as you grieve and heal. In fact, we also recommend that you find someone—perhaps a trusted friend, a pastor, or a counselor—who can review the steps toward healing with you. Who could you turn to and trust with your story?

_____

_____

_____

Don't put off this part of the plan. Having a competent confidant in this process is essential to helping you move beyond your pain and get a fresh start. You can get rid of guilt and find personal renewal.

group discussion
on chapter seven

Sex, Lies, and the Great Escape

The following questions are to help facilitate a meaningful small-group discussion. Feel free to explore different territory, but don't veer too far off track. In the space provided, jot down some of the group's responses to these questions. And remember, anyone is always free to "pass" on any particular question without explanation.

1. Describe your experience of completing the exercises for this chapter. What did you learn about yourself?

_____

_____

_____

_____

2. On a one-to-ten scale, with one being "none" and ten being "a lot," how much control do you think we have over our sexual impulses and why?

_____

_____

_____

_____

3. Think back to the "compulsion for completion" concept discussed in chapter 1. How do you see this at play when it comes to our sexuality? How does our desire to be whole affect our sex lives? Does it differ for men and women, and if so, how?

_____

_____

_____

_____

4. Considering the five fundamental choices we have when it comes to having sex, which one makes the most sense to you and why? Have you, or do you know others who have fallen for unhealthy choices (e.g., "if we're in love it can't be wrong")? Why are these choices so seductive?

_____

_____

_____

_____

5. What do you think about the whole idea of drawing a line when it comes to sexual behavior on a date? Is it reasonable to think that a couple can make a decision about how far they will go and then stick to it when the heat is on? Why or why not?

_____

_____

_____

_____

6. If you were explaining to another person a few good reasons to save sex for marriage, what would you say? What would you say to the person who was no longer a virgin and was wondering whether he could reclaim his sexual purity?

_____

_____

_____

_____

Sex, Lies, and the Great Escape

To explore more of what the Bible has to say about this topic, consider the following passages:

• 1 Corinthians 6:18–20 talks about the painful impact of unwise sexual involvement in relationships.

_____

_____

_____

_____

• Galatians 5:19–21 talks about the emptiness of self-centered sexuality.

_____

_____

_____

_____

• Song of Solomon 1:1–4 celebrates the joy of sex.

_____

_____

_____

_____

Other books that may be of interest to you on this topic include:

• *Addicted to "Love"* by Stephen Arterburn (Ann Arbor: Vine Books, 1991).
   Like drug addicts or alcoholics, "love" addicts get high from sex and romance, develop a tolerance for it, and need ever-greater doses to keep going. This book examines why this addiction is on the rise, what it looks like, who it afflicts, and what you can do if you are suffering from it.

- *Sex for Christians* by Lewis B. Smedes (Grand Rapids: Eerdmans, 1976, 1994).

  Considered one of the definitive statements on sex and sexuality from a Christian perspective, this book offers frank yet compassionate discussion that is at once refreshingly open-minded and strongly biblical. Smedes treats specific sexual issues for single persons, presenting plain-spoken yet responsible perspectives on such things as erotic fantasies, petting, and adultery.

- *Free to Love Again* by Dick Purnell (Nashville: Thomas Nelson, 1989).

  The battle for a purified life can be won, and this book shows you how. It deals compassionately, yet realistically, with the sensitive issues of wrong moral choices and gives powerful advice for personal renewal. You will discover the process of healing and guidelines for a healthy love relationship by following the "seven steps to freedom."

exercises

for

chapter eight

How to
Break Up
Without
Falling Apart

Is It Time to Break Up?

This exercise will take about ten minutes and will help you determine whether breaking up is a good idea in your situation.

The following list of reasons could all be arguably justifiable for causing a breakup. Take a moment to review these reasons and place a check mark next to any that apply to you and your relationship.

It may be time to break up if . . .

_____ The relationship is stifling you.

_____ The relationship is out of balance.

_____ You can't be yourself.

_____ You feel dominated and controlled.

_____ You've outgrown each other.

_____ You feel betrayed by his or her actions.

_____ You're more interested in someone else.

_____ Your values clash.

_____ You are waiting for your dating partner to change.

_____ This person doesn't help you become the kind of person you want to be.

_____ You don't feel physically safe around this person.

_____ You don't feel emotionally safe around this person.

_____ You give more than you receive in the relationship.

_____ You feel disrespected by this person.

_____ Your dating partner is involved in unhealthy behavior (e.g., drug abuse).

_____ You feel pressured by him or her to be someone you're not.

If you checked one or more of the items in this list, you need to carefully consider whether it is time to break up and move on. Consulting with an objective friend or counselor may help you clarify your thinking and make up your mind.

Making a Clean Break

This exercise will take about ten minutes and will help you clarify your own thinking on initiating a breakup.

Consider the situation: You've dated this person for more than a year and have discovered that your values clash and that you are feeling stifled by the relationship. You want to break up. From the following options, which response would you most likely choose?

_____ "What do you think about us just being friends?"

_____ "I really like you, but I need some time to think about our relationship."

_____ "I'm not comfortable in this relationship anymore and think it's better if we don't see each other."

The choice you made—understandably forced—in the above scenario may give you a quick glimpse into your general predisposition toward breaking up. If you chose the first response you are probably most likely to skirt the issue and end up with a painful, drawn-out breakup. If you chose the second response, you are probably aware of what you need to do but very hesitant to make a clean break. The final choice, though difficult to say, is probably the one that helps both of you make a clean break and move on.

Whatever your choice in the above situation, the following questions will help you explore issues that may give you personal insight into making you a better "breaker-upper."

What is your biggest fear about initiating a breakup?

_____

_____

_____

Considering your situation, what is your idea of an ideal breakup? What would you say and how would it turn out?

_____

_____

_____

Avoiding the Blame Game

This exercise will take about ten minutes and will help you assess the degree to which you may be blaming yourself for your breakup. Consider each of the following statements and use the scale to indicate how often each represents your thoughts. Take your time and be as honest as you can.

1 — Rarely or none of the time
2 — A little of the time
3 — Some of the time
4 — A good part of the time
5 — Most or all of the time

_____ I believe I could have done a lot more to prevent the breakup.
_____ I believe I am responsible for the breakup.
_____ I worry about what this person thinks of me.
_____ I need to take a hard look at myself.
_____ I feel ashamed as a result of the breakup.
_____ I detest myself for allowing the breakup to happen.
_____ I think that if I changed I could win this person back.
_____ I blame myself for the breakup.
_____ I keep thinking about how I could have done things differently.
_____ I wish I could turn back time and do things differently.

Total Score x 2 = _____

Scoring: Add up your item scores and multiply your total by two. This provides a possible maximum score of up to 100. Use the following to interpret your score.

90–100 You are wracked with feelings of self-blame and punishment over being "rejected" by this person. You could probably benefit from help from a professional counselor to help you see reality more objectively in order to move beyond your pain.

80–89 You may not be in immediate need of professional help, but you aren't out of the danger zone. You need to process your feelings with a trusted friend or counselor and recognize the potential you have to suffer from serious self-punishment.

10–79 You are on your way to escaping the guilt trap. While your twinges of self-punishment are no doubt painful, you are most likely experiencing the common and natural feelings that many have after suffering a breakup. You will want to take special care not to allow self-blame to fester when it does appear.

Moving On

This exercise can take about ten minutes to much longer, and it will help you move beyond your grief of experiencing your breakup.

Take a moment to review the section of this chapter in the book that outlines Elisabeth Kübler-Ross's steps of grief and loss. In the space provided below, note how you have or are experiencing each phase. Write about your feelings during these times, and note some specific examples of what you experienced during each of them.

Denial

_____

_____

_____

_____

Anger

_____

_____

_____

_____

Bargaining

_____

_____

_____

_____

Depression

_____

_____

_____

_____

Acceptance

_____

_____

_____

_____

How to Break Up
Without Falling Apart

The following questions are to help facilitate a meaningful small-group discussion. Feel free to explore different territory, but don't veer too far off track. In the space provided, jot down some of the group's responses to these questions. And remember, anyone is always free to "pass" on any particular question without explanation.

1. Describe your experience of completing the exercises for this chapter. What did you learn about yourself?

   _____

   _____

   _____

2. What have you learned from watching others go through breakups? What have you witnessed that seemed to make sense, and what would you say would be good to avoid?

   _____

   _____

   _____

3. Can you think of a time when you stayed in an unhappy relationship (of any kind) because of the security it provided? What allowed you to finally move on?

   _____

   _____

   _____

4. As the initiator of a breakup, what would you do to make the split less painful for the person you are leaving?

_____

_____

_____

5. As the person on the receiving end of a breakup, what would you personally do to keep your self-esteem intact?

_____

_____

_____

6. Of all the phases one can expect to experience after a breakup (denial, anger, bargaining, depression, and acceptance), which one do you think is most important and why?

_____

_____

_____

How to Break Up Without Falling Apart

To explore more of what the Bible has to say about this topic, consider the following passages:

- Psalm 34:18 tells of God's compassion for the brokenhearted.

_____

_____

_____

- Psalm 69:20 voices the anguish of feelings that no one understands the pain of a broken heart.

_____

_____

_____

- Psalm 102:23–28 tells of God's consistency even when everything else seems to be changing.

_____

_____

_____

Other books that may be of interest to you on this topic include:

- *Seven Secrets of a Healthy Dating Relationship* by Les Parrott (Kansas City: Beacon Hill, 1995).

    Whether you are looking for someone to date, already in a relationship, or even considering marriage, this book reveals seven powerful ways for both becoming a healthy person and finding the kind of person who can help you build a healthy relationship. This book reveals qualities you probably never even thought to look for in a dating partner. Each chapter is accompanied by a self-test that will reveal how well you are doing in pursuing some of the things that matter most for a successful dating relationship.

- *Love's Unseen Enemy* by Les Parrott (Grand Rapids: Zondervan, 1994).

    Too often efforts to build loving relationships are unwittingly sabotaged by an unseen enemy: guilt. Whether you are the heartbreaker or the brokenhearted in a "former" relationship, it's not unlikely that you are struggling with the emotion of guilt. It's almost inevitable. So if you are feeling a pinch on your conscience, this book will help you identify your "relationship style" and resolve the shame and self-punishment you may be experiencing.

exercises
for
chapter nine

Relating
to God
Without
Feeling Phony

Honest-to-Goodness Doubt

This exercise will take about ten minutes and will help you consider your faith and the degree to which you struggle with doubt. On the following continuums, circle the number that indicates where you stand. Be as honest in your responses as you can be.

My "faith" is nonexistent.   My faith is rock solid.

1   2   3   4   5   6   7   8   9   10

I don't know God.   I know God personally.

1   2   3   4   5   6   7   8   9   10

The Bible is just another book.   The Bible is a holy book inspired by God.

1   2   3   4   5   6   7   8   9   10

Jesus was simply an historical figure.   Jesus is my personal Savior.

1   2   3   4   5   6   7   8   9   10

God doesn't hear my prayers.   God hears and answers my prayers.

1   2   3   4   5   6   7   8   9   10

As you consider where you stand on the above continuums, take a moment to summarize your faith in a single sentence.

_____

_____

Now take a moment to summarize your doubt in a single sentence.

_____

_____

Will the Real God Please Stand Up?

This exercise can take about ten minutes and will help you uncover any misconceptions or distorted beliefs you have about God. Take a moment to review the passage in this chapter that ponders the question "Who is God?" Consider the four distorted concepts of God that are mentioned and indicate how often you view God in these ways.

	Rarely	Sometimes	Often
The Referee God	___	___	___
The Grandfather God	___	___	___
The Scientist God	___	___	___
The Bodyguard God	___	___	___

From the above list of distortions, which one are you most likely to view and why? If none of these four distortions is likely to trip you up, how do you sometimes misunderstand God's character?

_____

_____

_____

Now consider what may be one of the most difficult questions you have ever pondered: Who is God to you? Take a moment to write a brief paragraph on this topic. Consider the traits and qualities that come to mind when you think about who God is.

_____

_____

_____

_____

_____

_____

_____

Does God Really Love Me?

This exercise will take about ten minutes and will help you assess the degree to which you experience God's love at a personal level. Consider each of the following statements and use the scale to indicate how often each represents your beliefs. Take your time and be as honest as you can.

1 — Rarely or none of the time
2 — A little of the time
3 — Some of the time
4 — A good part of the time
5 — Most or all of the time

____ I believe that nothing could ever separate me from God's love.
____ I am aware of how special I am to God.
____ I believe that God is love.
____ God's grace permeates my life.
____ I'm confident that God loves me so much that he sacrificed his only Son in my place.
____ I believe God loves me as if I were the only person on earth.
____ I am free from irrational guilt feelings because of God's love.
____ I believe I can do nothing to earn God's love because it is given freely.
____ I know God loves me.
____ I can love others because God first loved me.

Total Score x 2 = ____

Scoring: Add up your item scores and multiply your total by two. This provides a possible maximum score of up to 100. Use the following to interpret your score.

90–100 You have a solid and secure understanding of how much God loves you.

80–89 You may experience some ambivalence at times about how much God loves you, but deep down you rest in knowing that he does love you.

10–79 You are struggling to know whether God loves you or not. If your score is below 60, you would certainly benefit from counsel on God's grace.

exercise thirty-six

Really Relating to God

This exercise can take as little as ten minutes to much longer, and it is designed to help you formulate how you relate to God and how you wish you related to God—and what you can do to move in that direction. This final workbook exercise may appear relatively simple at first, but it is probably the most difficult of all.

In a single sentence, summarize your faith journey and how it has brought you to your present relationship with God. Then note a few key descriptors of your present relationship with God.

_____

_____

_____

_____

Now, take a moment to consider how you might represent your present relationship with God by drawing a simple picture of it. Be as creative as you like.

Once you have completed your pictorial representation of this relationship, consider what you would like to change to make it more like the relationship you long for. What would those changes involve?

_____

_____

_____

_____

What can you do, in practical terms, to make that kind of relationship with God a reality?

_____

_____

_____

_____

Relating to God
Without Feeling Phony

The following questions are to help facilitate a meaningful small-group discussion. Feel free to explore different territory, but don't veer too far off track. In the space provided, jot down some of the group's responses to these questions. And remember, anyone is always free to "pass" on any particular question without explanation.

1. Describe your experience of completing the exercises for this chapter. What did you learn about yourself?

_____

_____

_____

_____

2. Does doubt have any place in an authentic relationship with God? Why or why not? Do you believe that God can help a person find a faith of her own? If so, how?

_____

_____

_____

_____

3. The chapter mentions a few misperceptions people often have about who God is. Do you identify with any of these? If so, how? If not, what misperceptions of God's character have you experienced?

_____

_____

_____

_____

4. If someone were to ask you why a person needs God, what would you say and why?

_____

_____

_____

_____

5. In specific terms, how do you see God as the only one who can truly fulfill our compulsion for completion? If you don't agree with this position, why not?

_____

_____

_____

_____

6. What does it mean to you when this chapter says the only way to relate to God without feeling phony is to do so with integrity? What does integrity mean to you?

_____

_____

_____

_____

Relating to God
Without Feeling Phony

To explore more of what the Bible has to say about this topic consider the following passages:

• Ephesians 3:16–19 talks about the experience of knowing God deeply.

_____

_____

• Psalm 139 talks about the intimate way God knows us.

_____

_____

• John 15:1–15 talks about the intimate relationship we have with God through Christ.

_____

_____

Other books that may be of interest to you on this topic include:

• *The Jesus I Never Knew* by Philip Yancey (Grand Rapids: Zondervan, 1995).
  This award-winning book takes an honest look at the Jesus described in the Gospels and brings the author to conclude: "The Jesus I got to know in writing this book is very different from the Jesus I learned about in Sunday school. In some ways he is more comforting; in some ways more terrifying." Yancey offers a new and different perspective on the life of Christ. Covering everything from the manger in Bethlehem to the cross in Jerusalem, Yancey presents a complex character who generates questions

as well as answers, and a disturbing and exhilarating Jesus who wants to radically transform your life and stretch your faith.

- *Finding God* by Larry Crabb (Grand Rapids: Zondervan, 1993).

    In today's psychological culture, according to Crabb, we have become a people more concerned with solving our problems than finding God. But solving problems is not the point. In fact, whenever we place higher priority on solving our problems than on pursuing God we miss out on our relationship with him. With this book, Dr. Crabb upsets the cozy Christianity of the modern believer. He reveals anew God's top priority: not your comfort and gratification, but his glory.

- *The God You're Looking For* by Bill Hybels (Nashville: Nelson, 1997).

    To find God, according to Bill Hybels, you'll first need to put aside the caricatures, the fears, the lies, and the misconceptions that have been gathered over the centuries about who God really is. Understanding the true personality and nature of God can make ordinary people extraordinary and weak people strong. With penetrating insights and pointed anecdotes, Hybels reveals God for who he really is: A God who feels your joy and sadness, a God who doesn't stop giving, a God who has your life in his loving hands.

Love's Unseen Enemy

How to Overcome Guilt to Build Healthy Relationships

Dr. Les Parrott III

Too often efforts to build loving relationships are unwittingly sabotaged by an unseen enemy: guilt. In *Love's Unseen Enemy*, Dr. Les Parrott shows how to build healthier relationships by overcoming the feelings of false guilt and by dealing forthrightly with true guilt.

Dr. Parrott identifies the four relationship styles created by the combination of love and guilt:

- **Pleasers** love with their hearts, not their heads. They do loving things to relieve their guilt.
- **Controllers** can identify the problems with their minds, but don't always exude warmth and love.
- **Withholders** carry their guilt but are afraid to love.
- **Lovers** have learned to tap their capacity for genuine empathy. They strive to be loving, not simply to do loving things.

Parrott shows how your relational style affects your friendships, your marriage, your children, your work, and your relationship with God. Look for *Love's Unseen Enemy* at your local Christian bookstore.

Hardcover 0-310-40150-X
Mass Market Paperback 0-06-100940-7

ZondervanPublishingHouse
Grand Rapids, Michigan 49530
http://www.zondervan.com

Saving Your Marriage Before It Starts

Seven Questions to Ask Before (and After) You Marry

Drs. Les & Leslie Parrott III

Did you know many couples spend more time preparing for their wedding than they do for their marriage?

Having tasted firsthand the difficulties of "wedding bell blues," Drs. Les and Leslie Parrott show young couples the skills they need to make the transition from "single" to "married" smooth and enjoyable.

Saving Your Marriage Before It Starts is more than a book—it's practically a premarital counseling session. A few questions that will be explored are:

- Question 1: Have You Faced the Myths of Marriage with Honesty?
- Question 3: Have You Developed the Habit of Happiness?
- Question 6: Do You Know How to Fight a Good Fight?

Questions at the end of every chapter help you explore each topic personally. Companion men's and women's workbooks full of self-tests and exercises will help you apply what you learn. And the *Saving Your Marriage Before It Starts* video curriculum will help you to learn and grow with other couples who are dealing with the same struggles and questions.

Here's what the experts are saying about *Saving Your Marriage Before It Starts:*

"I've spent the past twenty-five years developing material to strengthen marriages. I wish *Saving Your Marriage Before It Starts* had been developed years ago."

H. Norman Wright
Author of *Before You Say I Do*

"The Parrotts have a unique way of capturing fresh insights from research and then showing the practical implications from personal experience. This is one of the few 'must read' books on marriage."

Dr. David Stoop, Clinical Psychologist,
Cohost of the New Life Clinics Radio Program

WINNER OF
THE 1996 ECPA GOLD MEDALLION BOOK AWARDS

Hardcover 0-310-49240-8
Audio Pages 0-310-49248-3
Video Curriculum 0-310-20451-8
Workbook for Men 0-310-48731-5
Workbook for Women 0-310-48741-2